Connections!

PEOPLE

CAROLINE GRIMSHAW

TEXT **IQBAL HUSSAIN**

SCIENCE CONSULTANT **JOHN STRINGER**

HUMANITIES CONSULTANT **RICHARD RIESER**
DISABILITY EQUALITY IN EDUCATION

ILLUSTRATIONS **NICK DUFFY** ☆ **SPIKE GERRELL** ☆ **JO MOORE**

TWO-CAN
IN ASSOCIATION WITH
WATTS BOOKS

Connections!

PEOPLE

CREATIVE AND EDITORIAL DIRECTOR
CONCEPT/FORMAT/DESIGN
CAROLINE GRIMSHAW

TEXT **IQBAL HUSSAIN**

SCIENCE CONSULTANT **JOHN STRINGER**

HUMANITIES CONSULTANT **RICHARD RIESER**
DISABILITY EQUALITY IN EDUCATION

ILLUSTRATIONS
NICK DUFFY ☆ **SPIKE GERRELL** ☆ **JO MOORE**

THANKS TO
DEBBIE DORMAN PICTURE RESEARCH
JUSTINE COOPER AND **ROBERT SVED** EDITORIAL SUPPORT
AND **ANDREW JARVIS** ☆ **RUTH KING**
CHARLES SHAAR MURRAY ☆ **PAUL DU NOYER**

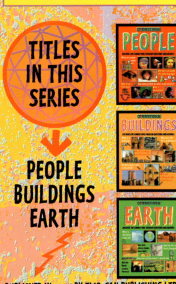

TITLES IN THIS SERIES

→

PEOPLE
BUILDINGS
EARTH

PUBLISHED IN 1995 BY TWO-CAN PUBLISHING LTD
IN ASSOCIATION WITH WATTS BOOKS,
96 LEONARD STREET, LONDON EC2A 4RH.
COPYRIGHT © TWO-CAN PUBLISHING LTD, 1995.
TWO-CAN PUBLISHING LTD,
346 OLD STREET, LONDON EC1V 9NQ.
PRINTED AND BOUND IN BELGIUM BY PROOST NV
EDITION NUMBER 2 4 6 8 10 9 7 5 3 1
ALL RIGHTS RESERVED. NO PART OF THIS PUBLICATION
MAY BE REPRODUCED, STORED IN A RETRIEVAL SYSTEM OR
TRANSMITTED IN ANY FORM OR BY ANY MEANS ELECTRONIC,
MECHANICAL, PHOTOCOPYING, RECORDING OR OTHERWISE,
WITHOUT PRIOR WRITTEN PERMISSION OF THE COPYRIGHT
OWNER. A CATALOGUE RECORD FOR THIS BOOK IS
AVAILABLE FROM THE BRITISH LIBRARY.
ISBN 1-85434-319-X (PB) ISBN 1-85434-284-3 (HB)

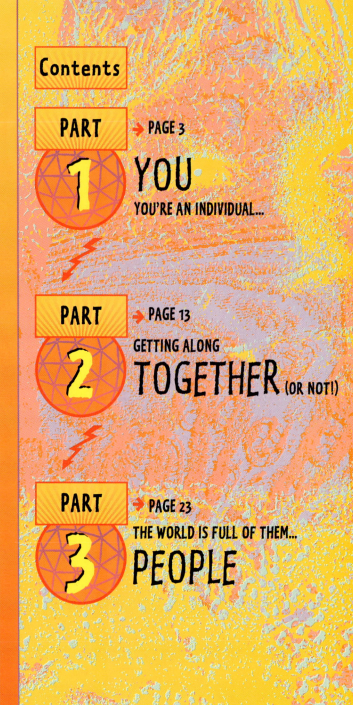

Contents

PART **1** → PAGE 3
YOU
YOU'RE AN INDIVIDUAL...

PART **2** → PAGE 13
GETTING ALONG
TOGETHER (OR NOT!)

PART **3** → PAGE 23
THE WORLD IS FULL OF THEM...
PEOPLE

DISCOVER THE CONNECTIONS THROUGH QUESTIONS AND ANSWERS...
YOU CAN READ THIS BOOK FROM START TO FINISH OR LEAP-FROG THROUGH THE SECTIONS FOLLOWING THE PATHS SUGGESTED IN THESE SPECIAL 'CONNECT!' BOXES.

Connect!

ENJOY YOUR JOURNEY OF DISCOVERY AND UNDERSTANDING

Yes,

YOU,

you're an individual...

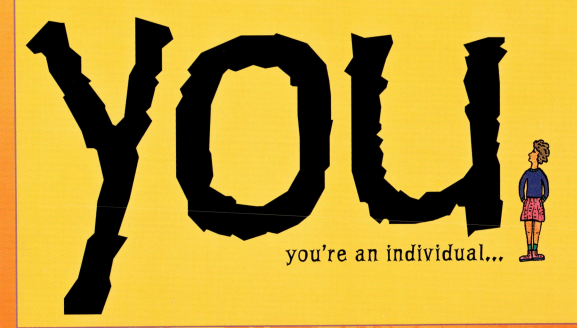

What are genes, and how do they make individuals unique?

Why does the body grow?

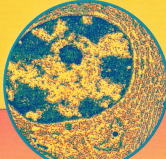

What is a genius?

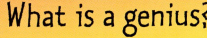
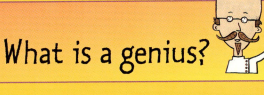

You'll find all these questions (and more!)
answered in PART ONE of your journey of discovery
and understanding. Turn the page! ---✈

SO YOU WANT TO KNOW WHAT PEOPLE ARE ALL ABOUT? READ ON!

QUESTION 1

What makes people unique?

The answer lies in our genes. These are special instructions found in our cells when we are born.

Genes are responsible for how we look. They explain why tall parents often have tall children, and why brothers and sisters sometimes look alike. We have one set of genes, half from each parent. Among other things, genes decide our hair colour, whether we have ear lobes or not and even the shape of our bodies!

EYE COLOUR IS DETERMINED BY THE PAIR OF GENES GIVEN TO US BY OUR PARENTS. THE GENE FOR BROWN EYES IS DOMINANT, WHICH MEANS THAT ONE BROWN GENE IN THE PAIR IS ENOUGH TO GIVE YOU BROWN EYES. THE BLUE GENE IS SAID TO BE RECESSIVE. SO YOU ONLY GET BLUE EYES IF BOTH GENES ARE BLUE.

Prove It!

Can you roll your tongue lengthways? If not, the chances are that both your parents can't either!

☆ **WHAT ABOUT TWINS?**

The most common types of twins are:

1 **IDENTICAL** THE EGG CONTAINING THE BABY SPLITS INTO TWO DURING PREGNANCY. EACH EGG CARRIES IDENTICAL GENETIC INFORMATION, WHICH IS WHY THE BABIES LOOK ALMOST EXACTLY THE SAME. ALTHOUGH IDENTICAL TWINS LOOK SIMILAR, THEY STILL HAVE DIFFERENT FINGERPRINT PATTERNS.

2 **FRATERNAL** TWO EGGS SLIP INTO THE MOTHER'S WOMB AND BOTH DEVELOP INTO BABIES. THESE TWINS DO NOT LOOK THE SAME, BECAUSE THEY HAVE NOT SPLIT FROM THE SAME EGG.

QUESTION 2

But, how are people different?

We all look different. We may be the same under the skin, but our faces show lots of variation.

SOME PEOPLE HAVE DISTINGUISHING MARKS, SUCH AS BIRTHMARKS AND BEAUTY SPOTS. DO YOU?

HAIR
STRAIGHT, CURLY, SHORT, LONG, BLACK, BLONDE, STRAWBERRY.
HAIR GROWS OUT OF TINY HOLES IN YOUR SKIN.
ROUND HOLES = STRAIGHT HAIR
OVAL HOLES = WAVY HAIR
OBLONG HOLES = CURLY HAIR

SKIN
FRECKLY, PALE, DARK, SMOOTH.
SKIN COLOUR DEPENDS ON A SUBSTANCE CALLED MELANIN. THE MORE MELANIN YOU HAVE, THE DARKER YOUR SKIN. IN THE SUN YOUR SKIN PRODUCES EXTRA MELANIN TO STOP YOU BURNING, AND YOU GET A TAN.

NOSE
STRAIGHT, CROOKED, FLAT, SMALL.
YOUR NOSE CAN DETECT UP TO 5,000 DIFFERENT SMELLS.

EYES
BLUE, BROWN, GREEN, HAZEL, GREY.
YOUR EYES CAN TELL THE DIFFERENCE BETWEEN TEN MILLION DIFFERENT SHADES OF COLOUR.

LIPS
THIN, THICK, PURSED, FULL.
YOUR LIPS ARE ONE OF THE MOST SENSITIVE PARTS OF YOUR BODY.

☆ **WHAT ARE THE CHANCES OF HUMAN MULTIPLE BIRTHS?**

TWINS (TWO CHILDREN) = 1 in 89.
TRIPLETS (THREE CHILDREN) = 1 in 7,900.
QUADRUPLETS (FOUR CHILDREN) = 1 in 705,000.

Connect!

HOW YOU LOOK MAY AFFECT THE WAY PEOPLE THINK ABOUT YOU. WANT TO KNOW MORE? THEN TURN TO Q46.

Why does the body grow?

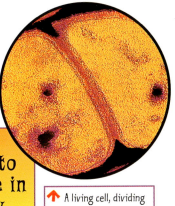

Our bodies are made up of millions of cells, which take food from the body, helping them to multiply and form new cells. It is the increase in the number of cells that makes the body grow.

 A living cell, dividing and multiplying.

Our bodies are all different shapes and sizes.

THERE ARE OVER 5,000 MILLION PEOPLE ON THE PLANET. EACH ONE HAS THEIR OWN UNIQUE SHAPE.

HERE ARE THE THREE MAIN BODY SHAPES

This girl is a model. She is thought to be glamorous because of her body shape and general physical appearance.

Sumo wrestling originated in Japan in around 23BC. These wrestlers work hard to maintain their weight and size.

1 ENDOMORPH
Well-rounded, heavy build.

2 MESOMORPH
Athletic, broad chest.

3 ECTOMORPH
Thin and tall.

Connect!
WHAT YOU EAT AFFECTS THE WAY YOU LOOK. Q7 EXPLAINS MORE.

We have our own unique fingerprints.

NO TWO PEOPLE HAVE EXACTLY THE SAME FINGERPRINT PATTERN. PRINTS CAN BE DIVIDED INTO THREE TYPES OR GROUPS. SOME PEOPLE BELIEVE THAT EACH TYPE OF PRINT HAS A CERTAIN MEANING.

ARCH = PRACTICAL AND CREATIVE.

LOOP = STEADY AND RELIABLE.

WHORL = INDIVIDUAL AND THOUGHTFUL.

Prove It!
Check out the fingerprints of your friends. Which pattern is the most common?

☆ HOW QUICKLY DOES THE BODY GROW?

An average baby weighs about 3.3kg when it is born. It doubles its weight in just over four months. You stop growing at around the age of 21, and actually start to shrink when you reach your fifties.

Better diet and fitness mean that today people are taller than they have ever been. In Britain, men are at least 8cm taller, on average, than they would have been only 50 years ago.

☆ AVERAGE HEIGHT		
	1945	1994
MEN	1.70m	1.78m
WOMEN	1.57m	1.65m

Connect!
HOW LONG DO PEOPLE LIVE? CHECK OUT Q10.

QUESTION

4 What are people made of?

The body is made up of billions of different parts, all of which fit together neatly to give us life. If you were making a human, these are the main ingredients you would need.

☆ INGREDIENTS FOR MAKING A HUMAN

1. 208 bones of various shapes and sizes
2. 650 assorted muscles
3. 5 million strands of hair
4. 100,000km of blood vessels
5. 6.5m of small intestine
6. 1.5m of long intestine
7. Between 5 and 6 litres of blood
8. 80km of nerves
9. Selection of organs, for example: heart, lungs, kidneys, brain
10. A dash of hormones
11. Skin to cover

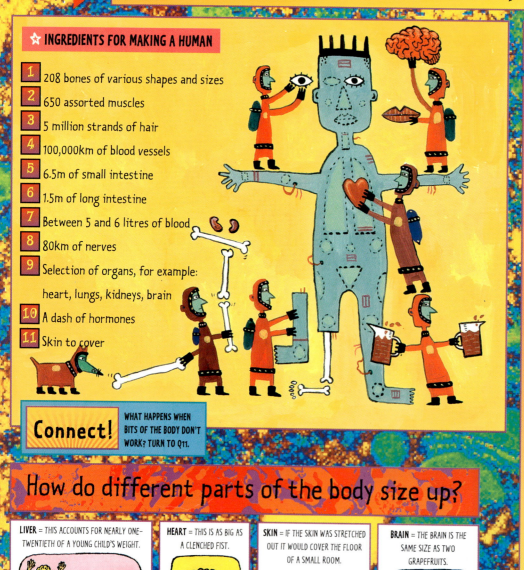

Connect! WHAT HAPPENS WHEN BITS OF THE BODY DON'T WORK? TURN TO Q11.

Body breakdown

Like all living things, humans are mainly made of fats, proteins and carbohydrates. On top of that, a surprising two-thirds of the body is made from water!

☆ THIS BODY IS MADE UP OF...

WATER	65%
PROTEIN	18%
FAT	10%
CARBOHYDRATE	5%
OTHERS	2%

There are other chemicals present in the body, but in much smaller amounts.

 PHOSPHORUS = HELPS TURN ENERGY INTO MOVEMENT.

 IRON = HELPS CARRY OXYGEN AROUND THE BODY.

 COBALT = PROTECTS AGAINST A DISEASE CALLED ANAEMIA.

 CALCIUM = STRENGTHENS BONES AND TEETH.

How do different parts of the body size up?

LIVER = THIS ACCOUNTS FOR NEARLY ONE-TWENTIETH OF A YOUNG CHILD'S WEIGHT.

HEART = THIS IS AS BIG AS A CLENCHED FIST.

SKIN = IF THE SKIN WAS STRETCHED OUT IT WOULD COVER THE FLOOR OF A SMALL ROOM.

BRAIN = THE BRAIN IS THE SAME SIZE AS TWO GRAPEFRUITS.

Connect! HOW DO WE TAKE SOME OF THESE NUTRIENTS INTO OUR BODIES? TURN TO Q7.

QUESTION 5

But, what really makes us tick?

The computer in your head – your amazing brain!

☆ WHAT DOES THE BRAIN LOOK LIKE?

THIS!

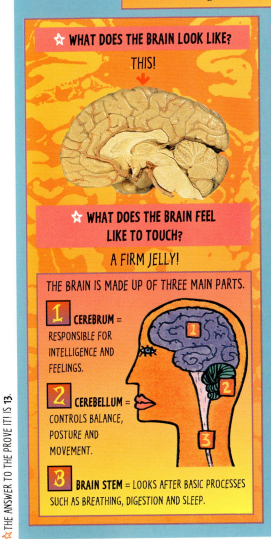

☆ WHAT DOES THE BRAIN FEEL LIKE TO TOUCH?

A FIRM JELLY!

THE BRAIN IS MADE UP OF THREE MAIN PARTS.

1 CEREBRUM = RESPONSIBLE FOR INTELLIGENCE AND FEELINGS.

2 CEREBELLUM = CONTROLS BALANCE, POSTURE AND MOVEMENT.

3 BRAIN STEM = LOOKS AFTER BASIC PROCESSES SUCH AS BREATHING, DIGESTION AND SLEEP.

☆ HOW DOES THE BRAIN WORK?

Your brain is the operations centre of your entire body, controlling everything you do. It is made up of nerve cells which pass information down nerves to the body's muscles. The brain then receives these messages, or electronic impulses, and acts on them. Each bit of the brain is responsible for a particular job. The right side of your brain controls the left side of your body, while the left side of your brain controls the right side of your body.

Connect!

HEARING, TALKING, SEEING, SMELLING AND TOUCHING ARE ALL SENSES. BUT HOW DO WE SHOW OUR FEELINGS? TURN TO Q23.

DIFFERENT BRAIN AREAS ARE RESPONSIBLE FOR DIFFERENT ACTIONS

HEARING ▮ TALKING ▮ SEEING ▮

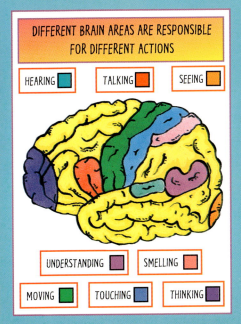

UNDERSTANDING ▮ SMELLING ▮

MOVING ▮ TOUCHING ▮ THINKING ▮

ALL ANIMALS HAVE SOME KIND OF BRAIN. THE MORE DEVELOPED THE ANIMAL, THE BIGGER THE BRAIN.

SHARKS AND FISH HAVE SIMPLE BRAINS.

CEREBRUM IS LARGER IN BIRDS AND REPTILES.

MAMMALS HAVE THE MOST WELL-DEVELOPED BRAINS.

THE MOST HUMAN-LIKE BRAIN BELONGS TO THE APE.

☆ THE ANSWER TO THE PROVE IT! IS **13**.

Connect!

WHAT HAVE HUMANS DEVELOPED TO HELP THEM COMMUNICATE? TURN TO Q33.

QUESTION 6

What is a genius?

They were! ↓

ALBERT EINSTEIN (1879–1955) SCIENTIST: FAMOUS FOR HIS THEORY OF RELATIVITY.

LEONARDO DA VINCI (1452–1519) SCIENTIST AND ARTIST: FAMOUS FOR PAINTING THE 'MONA LISA'.

THERE IS NO LINK BETWEEN THE SIZE OF YOUR BRAIN AND HOW CLEVER YOU ARE. THE MOST COMMON WAY OF MEASURING INTELLIGENCE IS TO TAKE AN INTELLIGENCE QUOTIENT (IQ) TEST. THIS ASKS YOU TO SOLVE DIFFERENT TYPES OF PROBLEMS, INCLUDING ONES BASED ON MATHS AND LANGUAGE. THE AVERAGE SCORE IS 100 – TO BE A GENIUS, YOU NEED A SCORE OF MORE THAN 148.

Connect!

BEING A GENIUS CAN GIVE YOU FAME AND POWER. TURN TO Q25 TO FIND OUT MORE.

Prove It!

Try the following question from an IQ test. What comes next in the series? 1, 1, 2, 3, 5, 8, ? The answer is hidden on this page.

☆ SHAKUNTALA DEVI IS A HUMAN CALCULATOR! SHE ONCE MULTIPLIED TWO 13-DIGIT NUMBERS IN HER HEAD AND CAME UP WITH THE CORRECT ANSWER IN JUST 28 SECONDS.

QUESTION

7 Why do we need to eat food to stay alive?

Food keeps us warm, gives us energy and helps our bodies to stay in good condition.

How do we taste different flavours?

These are essential

FOOD CONTAINS FIVE ESSENTIAL NUTRIENTS:

1 CARBOHYDRATES A MAIN SOURCE OF ENERGY.

2 PROTEINS HELP THE BODY GROW AND REPAIR ITSELF.

3 VITAMINS KEEP THE BODY IN GOOD HEALTH.

4 FATS CONTAIN COMPONENTS THAT MAKE UP THE BODY, AND GIVE ENERGY.

5 MINERALS HELP THE BODY PARTS FUNCTION.

IS THERE ANYTHING ELSE?
YES, FIBRE, OR ROUGHAGE AS IT IS SOMETIMES CALLED. THIS IS FOOD WHICH HUMANS CANNOT DIGEST. INSTEAD IT PASSES STRAIGHT THROUGH THE BODY, HELPING IT TO GET RID OF WASTE.

Keeping it balanced

A balanced diet should supply you with all the nutrients you need to stay healthy. Doctors recommend cutting down on sugar and fat, and having more fruit and vegetables.

☆ GOOD TO INCREASE

LOW FAT PROTEINS (EG CHICKEN, FISH, BEANS AND PULSES)

FRUIT AND VEGETABLES

GRAINS, RICE AND CEREALS

☆ GOOD TO DECREASE

HIGH FAT PROTEINS (EG RED MEAT)

FATS AND DAIRY PRODUCTS

SUGARY FOODS

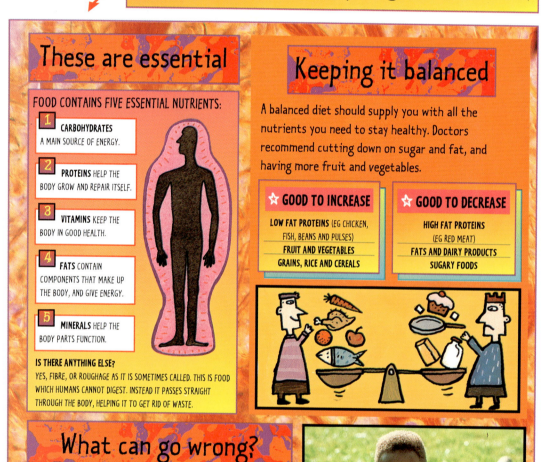

Taste buds are scattered all over the tongue. There are concentrations of different types of bud on different areas of the tongue. You sense bitter tastes better at the back of your tongue, sugary foods at the tip, salt at the sides, and sour foods with the middle sides of your tongue.

⬆ This a close-up picture of the surface of the tongue.

What can go wrong?

Too much or too little of one kind of food can seriously affect a person's health. Take a look at these examples.

☆ NOT ENOUGH OF...

NUTRIENT: VITAMIN C
FOUND: CITRUS FRUITS, GREEN VEGETABLES

☆ CAN GIVE YOU...

SCURVY

☆ TOO MUCH OF...

NUTRIENT: FAT
FOUND: DAIRY PRODUCTS AND OILS

☆ CAN GIVE YOU...

ALL THE CONDITIONS YOU NEED FOR A HEART ATTACK

⬆ Eating the right foods can make the skin, eyes and teeth more healthy.

Connect!

PEOPLE IN DIFFERENT PARTS OF THE WORLD ENJOY VERY DIFFERENT FOODS. CHECK OUT Q43.

Prove It!

Discover your different taste bud areas by dabbing various bitter, salty, sweet and sour foods around your tongue.

How long can the body last without food?

About three weeks. Sometimes people decide to either eat less, or stop eating food, for a short period. This is called **fasting**.

☆ WHY DO PEOPLE FAST?

1 To allow the body to get rid of unwanted chemicals, or toxins.

2 To bring attention to themselves or a particular cause.

3 As a religious act. This may be a way for worshippers to cleanse their bodies, ask for forgiveness, grieve or take their minds away from physical things and focus on their religion.

☆ WHO FASTS AND WHEN?

JEWS = YOM KIPPUR (DAY OF ATONEMENT), EIGHT DAYS AFTER THE JEWISH NEW YEAR.

CHRISTIANS = DURING THE 40 DAYS OF LENT, BEFORE THE EASTER FESTIVAL.

MUSLIMS = FROM SUNRISE TO SUNSET DURING THE MONTH OF RAMADAN, THE NINTH MONTH OF THE MUSLIM YEAR.

↑ As well as fasting, Muslims pray and read their holy book, the Koran.

Connect!

SOME PEOPLE LIVE IN COUNTRIES WHERE FOOD IS SCARCE. TO FIND OUT ABOUT FAMINE, TURN TO Q43.

QUESTION **8**

What else do we need to keep the body in good working order?

Take a look at this list of essentials for a healthy life.

1 SLEEP

Some scientists believe sleep allows the body time to repair itself. Others think it is a way of saving valuable energy. Whatever the reason, sleep is essential for survival. Going without sleep causes restlessness, hallucinations and blurred vision.

Californian Robert MacDonald holds the record for the longest period without any sleep – 18 days, 21 hours and 40 minutes.

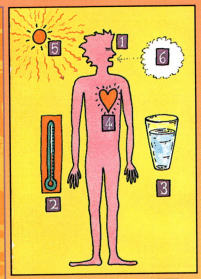

2 WARMTH

Humans are warm-blooded, which means that our body temperature remains fairly stable, no matter how cold or hot it is outside. But, we need to be careful of extreme changes in temperature.

TOO HOT	TOO COLD
CAUSES HEATSTROKE AND HEART ATTACKS.	CAUSES HYPOTHERMIA AND FROSTBITE.

↑ Eskimos can endure temperatures as low as –50°C. One reason is their diet, which is rich in protein and fat. The nutrients help to insulate their bodies from the cold.

4 LOVE

Everyone needs to be loved. Friendship and encouragement make us happier and help us to perform better, both physically and mentally.

3 WATER

During the day, the body loses water. If this isn't replaced, the body dehydrates. The longest you can survive without water is about four days.

THE BODY LOSES WATER
AS SWEAT, THROUGH PERSPIRATION.
AS WATER VAPOUR, THROUGH BREATHING.
AS URINE, THROUGH VISITING THE TOILET.

CASE STUDY

WHAT IF YOU RECEIVE NO LOVE? ONE YOUNG GIRL SPENT THE FIRST 13 YEARS OF HER LIFE LEFT FOR HOURS IN A SINGLE ROOM. SHE WAS TOLD TO KEEP QUIET AND WAS BEATEN IF SHE MADE A SOUND. WHEN SHE WAS DISCOVERED, SHE COULD NOT SPEAK OR WALK PROPERLY.

Connect!

TURN TO Q24 TO FIND OUT WHAT LOVE IS ALL ABOUT.

Prove It!

The next time someone praises you, make a note of how you feel. What are your feelings when you're being told off?

5 LIGHT

Sunlight triggers a part of the brain called the pineal gland. This can bring feelings of pleasure, which is why people may feel happier on sunny days. In winter, the light isn't as intense and it gets darker earlier. There is less stimulation of the pineal gland.

6 OXYGEN

Without the gas oxygen, the body would collapse after just a few minutes. Food burns with oxygen to create energy. This lets the body carry out its functions.

Connect!

HOW CAN AIR SERIOUSLY DAMAGE OUR HEALTH? TURN TO Q10.

9 Why do we get sick?

Sometimes the human body fails to work properly. One reason why a body may become sick is if it does not receive a healthy, balanced diet. The body is also under constant attack from hundreds of different germs.

What is a germ?

The two main kinds of germs, or microbes, are bacteria and viruses. These tiny organisms are responsible for most human diseases. Bacteria can grow and reproduce outside living cells. Viruses can only reproduce inside a living cell.

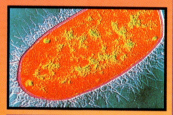

↑ This is a highly-magnified photograph of bacteria. If a hundred bacteria were laid end to end they would only be as big as this full stop.

SOME BACTERIAL DISEASES:
PNEUMONIA, CHOLERA, TYPHOID.
SOME VIRAL DISEASES:
INFLUENZA, CHICKENPOX.

Prove It!

Bacteria thrive in wet conditions. Leave two pieces of bread in polythene bags. Keep one wet and the other dry. Which piece goes mouldy first?

The body under attack

Germs invade our bodies in several ways.

CUTS AND SCRATCHES
A PRICK FROM A RUSTY NAIL CAN CAUSE TETANUS.

BREATHING IN
COLD AND FLU DROPLETS ENTER THROUGH THE NOSE AND MOUTH.

INSECT BITES
THE FEMALE MOSQUITO SPREADS MALARIA BY PIERCING A PERSON'S SKIN.

FOOD AND DRINK
ROTTEN EGGS AND MEAT CARRY SALMONELLA BUGS WHICH CAUSE FOOD POISONING.

10 How do we fight disease?

One litre of air contains about a million bacteria. We breathe in air all the time, yet rarely fall ill. This is because most of the microbes are harmless. But sometimes our bodies are not able to fight back and need medical help. There are two main weapons against disease.

1 **ANTIBIOTICS** ARE CHEMICAL SUBSTANCES WHICH KILL BACTERIA. PENICILLIN, ONE OF THE EARLIEST ANTIBIOTICS, WAS DISCOVERED BY ACCIDENT IN 1928. SCOTTISH SCIENTIST ALEXANDER FLEMING WAS GROWING BACTERIA IN A DISH WHEN HE SPOTTED SOME MOULD WHICH HAD BLOWN IN THROUGH THE WINDOW. HE NOTICED THAT THE BACTERIA WERE KILLED OFF WHEREVER THE MOULD WAS GROWING. THE MOULD FORMED THE BASIS OF PENICILLIN.

2 **VACCINES** ARE SMALL, WEAK DOSES OF A VIRUS WHICH ARE INJECTED INTO A PERSON. THE BODY THEN PRODUCES SPECIAL CHEMICALS CALLED ANTIBODIES TO FIGHT THE WEAK VIRUS. BY BEING VACCINATED, OR IMMUNISED, THE PERSON BECOMES RESISTANT TO THE VIRUS. IN FUTURE, THE BODY WILL QUICKLY PRODUCE THE SAME ANTIBODIES AGAIN TO TACKLE THE STRONGER, REAL VIRUS WITHOUT ANY ILL EFFECTS.

Connect!

WHEN A LARGE PART OF THE COMMUNITY IS AFFECTED BY A DISEASE, THIS IS CALLED A PLAGUE. PEOPLE MAY THEN UPROOT AND LEAVE THEIR HOMES. SEE Q39.

✱ THANKS TO A WORLD IMMUNISATION PROGRAMME, THE DISEASE SMALLPOX HAS BEEN COMPLETELY WIPED OUT.

★ AFTER THIS EXPERIMENT THROW AWAY BOTH BAGS UNOPENED.

What happens when parts of the body don't work?

AROUND 15% OF ALL PEOPLE HAVE A DISABILITY.

Some people are born with disabilities which give them mental or physical difficulties. Others have accidents or illnesses leaving them with a permanent loss of function.

WHEN YOU MEET SOMEONE, DO YOU DECIDE, JUST BY LOOKING AT THEM, WHAT THAT PERSON IS CAPABLE OF DOING?

THEY MAY BE BLIND OR DEAF PEOPLE. THEY MIGHT USE A WHEELCHAIR TO MOVE AROUND OR HAVE A LEARNING DIFFICULTY.

☆ HOW DO PEOPLE BECOME BLIND?

- THEY COULD BE BLIND FROM BIRTH DUE TO AN INFECTION IN THEIR MOTHER'S WOMB.
- THEY MAY HAVE FAILING EYESIGHT BECAUSE OF OLD AGE.
- PARTS OF THE EYE FAIL TO WORK PROPERLY, SUCH AS A DAMAGED OPTIC NERVE OR A DETACHED RETINA – THE LIGHT-SENSITIVE LAYER LINING THE BACK OF THE EYEBALL.

TO DEAL WITH THEIR DIFFICULTIES...

- THEY MAY USE THEIR SENSE OF SMELL, TOUCH, HEARING AND TASTE MORE EFFECTIVELY.
- THEY CAN READ BY TOUCHING PAGES WRITTEN IN RAISED LETTERS CALLED BRAILLE.
- SPECIALLY-TRAINED GUIDE DOGS ACT AS THE PERSON'S EYES.

☆ HOW DO PEOPLE BECOME DEAF?

- THE EARDRUM, OR SENSITIVE PART OF THE EAR CALLED THE COCHLEA, MAY BE DAMAGED.
- THEY MAY BE DEAF FROM BIRTH BECAUSE THEIR MOTHER HAD GERMAN MEASLES WHILE PREGNANT.

TO DEAL WITH THEIR DIFFICULTIES...

- THEY MAY WEAR A HEARING-AID TO MAKE SOUNDS LOUDER.
- THEY LEARN TO LIP-READ.
- THEY CAN LEARN TO COMMUNICATE BY USING A SYSTEM OF HAND GESTURES CALLED SIGN LANGUAGE.

THIS MAN IS A BRILLIANT SCIENTIST AND WORLD-FAMOUS AUTHOR. ALTHOUGH HE CAN'T SPEAK OR WALK, HE HAS A WAY OF COMMUNICATING HIS IDEAS TO THE WORLD.

⬆ PROFESSOR STEPHEN HAWKING has motor neurone disease, which is a muscle-wasting condition. He communicates by selecting letters, one at a time, from a computer screen. The computer then electronically 'speaks' the words.

☆ HOW LONG DO PEOPLE LIVE?

Life expectancy is the number of years that a child born today will be expected to live. Better healthcare and diet mean that nowadays people are living longer. Average life expectancy has increased from just 26 years during the time of the Roman Empire to 76 years today.

YEAR	LIFE EXPECTANCY
1870	42
1890	46
1910	54
1930	62
1950	67
1970	69
1990	72
TODAY	76

Connect! HOW ELSE, OTHER THAN BY SPEAKING, CAN WE COMMUNICATE HOW WE FEEL? SEE Q33.

Connect! IN POORER COUNTRIES, MORE CHILDREN DIE YOUNG BECAUSE OF DISEASE AND FAMINE. WHAT EFFECT DOES THIS HAVE ON THE SIZE OF THE FAMILY? SEE Q17.

Can we make a human?

Not yet. But...

TRANSPLANT SURGERY
DOCTORS CAN REPLACE DAMAGED PARTS OF THE BODY WITH HEALTHY ONES. THIS IS KNOWN AS TRANSPLANT SURGERY. THE NEW ORGANS ARE USUALLY TAKEN FROM SOMEONE WHO HAS RECENTLY DIED. ALMOST EVERY PART OF THE BODY CAN BE TRANSPLANTED – FROM THE LIVER, LUNGS AND HEART TO BONE MARROW AND EVEN BRAIN TISSUE.

ARTIFICIAL BODY PARTS ARE ALSO MADE TO REPLACE FAILED HUMAN PARTS

CERAMIC TEETH

GLASS EYES

ARTIFICIAL LIMBS

ARTIFICIAL ORGANS, SUCH AS AN ELECTRIC HEART PUMP

ARTIFICIAL BONES, EG THE HIP

Connect! HUMAN LIFE IS PRECIOUS, AND DOCTORS AND SCIENTISTS WORK HARD TO PRESERVE IT. WHAT HAPPENS WHEN HUMAN LIFE IS NOT CONSIDERED VALUABLE? SEE Q31.

QUESTION 13

What sort of choices do we make about ourselves?

Everyday we make decisions about what we wear and how we look generally. These decisions help to make us the individuals we are.

LET'S LOOK AT OUR OWN PERSONAL STYLE

Hairstyle

HOW WE WEAR OUR HAIR MAY DEPEND ON:
- The kind of hair we have and what suits us.
- Our personal taste and mood.
- What image we want to project.
- The fashion of the time.

1750s WOMEN HAD TOWERING HAIRSTYLES. SOME WERE AS TALL AS 60CM AND HAD TO BE SUPPORTED BY WIRE FRAMES.

1890s AMERICAN WOMEN WENT WILD OVER THE 'GIBSON GIRL' LOOK, A SOFT STYLE CREATED BY CHARLES GIBSON.

1940s HAIR WAS CUT INTO A SHORT STYLE CALLED THE 'BOB'. THIS LOOK BECAME POPULAR AGAIN IN THE LATE 1980s.

1970s FOLLOWERS OF PUNK FASHION MOULDED THEIR HAIR INTO ELABORATE BRIGHTLY-COLOURED 'MOHICAN-STYLE' SPIKES.

Clothes

WHAT INFLUENCES OUR CHOICE OF CLOTHES?
- The colour and style.
- Does it suit, or even flatter, us?
- Is it comfortable to wear?
- The price.

Connect!

SOME PEOPLE THINK THAT CERTAIN OCCASIONS REQUIRE SPECIAL CLOTHES. TURN TO Q18.

☆ A QUESTION OF TIMING

The height of fashion in one decade could be a fashion nightmare in the next.

⬆ In the 1970s, this was the height of fashion.

☆ A QUESTION OF CIRCUMSTANCE

In some countries, people dress in a particular way for religious reasons or as protection against the weather.

⬆ Arab women often wear a veil called a yashmak. They are advised in the Koran, the Muslim holy book, to be modest and cover their heads.

⬆ People in cold climates may wear fur clothes. These warm, insulated garments trap a layer of air to prevent body heat escaping.

QUESTION 14

What about the way we live?

We must also decide...
- WHAT TO EAT.
- HOW TO BEHAVE.
- HOW TO EARN A LIVING.
- WHAT TO DO WITH OUR TIME.
- WHO TO SHARE OUR TIME WITH.

How do people spend their time?

CLEANING TEETH 60 DAYS
SLEEPING 25 YEARS
EATING 2.5 YEARS
BLINKING 1.5 YEARS
EVERYTHING ELSE 25 YEARS
SITTING 20 YEARS

☆ **LIFETIME CLOCK** (HUMAN AGED 75)

Connect!

WHAT IS A FAMILY? TURN TO Q17.

Getting along

together

(or not!)

Why do we all speak different languages?

Why do people get married?

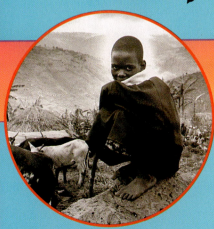

Why do we feel fear?

Do you want to find out the answers to these questions? Then turn the page and check out PART TWO. ----✈

15

When does a baby find out that there are other people in the world?

In the early part of its life, a baby simply responds to how it feels.

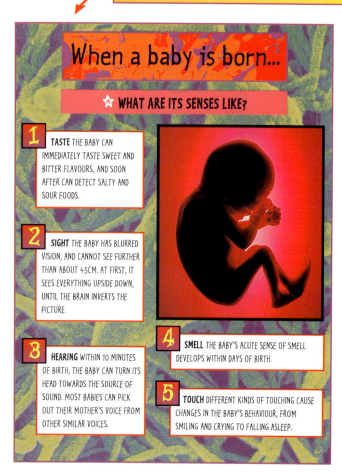

When a baby is born...

☆ WHAT ARE ITS SENSES LIKE?

1 **TASTE** THE BABY CAN IMMEDIATELY TASTE SWEET AND BITTER FLAVOURS, AND SOON AFTER CAN DETECT SALTY AND SOUR FOODS.

2 **SIGHT** THE BABY HAS BLURRED VISION, AND CANNOT SEE FURTHER THAN ABOUT 45CM. AT FIRST, IT SEES EVERYTHING UPSIDE DOWN, UNTIL THE BRAIN INVERTS THE PICTURE.

3 **HEARING** WITHIN 10 MINUTES OF BIRTH, THE BABY CAN TURN ITS HEAD TOWARDS THE SOURCE OF SOUND. MOST BABIES CAN PICK OUT THEIR MOTHER'S VOICE FROM OTHER SIMILAR VOICES.

4 **SMELL** THE BABY'S ACUTE SENSE OF SMELL DEVELOPS WITHIN DAYS OF BIRTH.

5 **TOUCH** DIFFERENT KINDS OF TOUCHING CAUSE CHANGES IN THE BABY'S BEHAVIOUR, FROM SMILING AND CRYING TO FALLING ASLEEP.

Charting the changes

WHEN DOES A CHILD LEARN TO RECOGNISE ITS SURROUNDINGS AND HOW DOES IT RESPOND?

THE AGE OF THE CHILD	WHAT DOES IT LEARN?
NEWBORN	CRYING ATTRACTS ITS PARENTS.
2 MONTHS	SMILING HOLDS PEOPLE'S ATTENTION.
3-6 MONTHS	SHOWS FONDNESS FOR PEOPLE APART FROM ITS PARENTS.
9-12 MONTHS	SPEAKS ONE OR TWO-WORD SENTENCES.
15-19 MONTHS	FEELS EMOTIONS, SUCH AS ANGER AND SADNESS.
2-3 YEARS	SHOWS INTEREST IN OTHER CHILDREN OF THE SAME AGE.

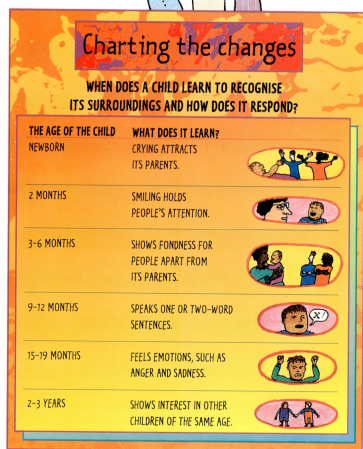

☆ PLAY IS IMPORTANT. IT SHOWS BABIES HOW TO BEHAVE WITH OTHERS, AND PREPARES THEM FOR THE ADULT WORLD.

Connect! WHAT HAPPENS WHEN A PERSON DECIDES NOT TO CONSIDER OTHERS? TURN TO Q31.

16

What is a relationship?

A relationship is how one person relates to, or is connected to, another person.

EACH PERSON HAS MANY DIFFERENT KINDS OF RELATIONSHIPS

PEOPLE MAY KNOW EACH OTHER BECAUSE...

THEY WORK TOGETHER, OR HAVE A BUSINESS RELATIONSHIP.

THEY ARE NEIGHBOURS, AND SEE EACH OTHER EVERY NOW AND AGAIN.

THEY LIKE, OR LOVE, EACH OTHER, AND BECOME GOOD FRIENDS.

THEY ARE A MEMBER OF THE SAME FAMILY.

What is a family?

AN 18TH-CENTURY RUSSIAN WOMAN HAD A RECORD-BREAKING 69 CHILDREN: 16 TWINS, SEVEN TRIPLETS AND FOUR QUADRUPLETS.

A family is a group of people linked to each other, for example by birth, marriage or adoption.

Some members of the family may share the activities of everyday life. Others may not. There are many different types of family unit. **STUDY THESE EXAMPLES.**

☆ NUCLEAR FAMILY

MOTHER, FATHER AND CHILDREN LIVING TOGETHER. SOMETIMES, AFTER DIVORCE OR A DEATH, A PARENT MAY REMARRY, CREATING A STEP-PARENT FAMILY.

☆ EXTENDED FAMILY

PARENTS, CHILDREN AND OTHER RELATIVES LIVING TOGETHER. THIS TYPE OF FAMILY IS COMMON IN THE MEDITERRANEAN, ASIA AND AFRICA.

☆ SINGLE-PARENT FAMILY

CHILDREN LIVING WITH ONE PARENT ONLY. THE NUMBER OF SINGLE-PARENT FAMILIES IS INCREASING, PARTICULARLY IN THE DEVELOPED WORLD.

☆ COMMUNE

GROUP OF PEOPLE LIVING TOGETHER BECAUSE THEY HAVE A SHARED INTEREST OR BELIEF. HIPPIES, GYPSIES AND MEMBERS OF SOME RELIGIONS LIVE IN COMMUNES.

WHY DO SOME CULTURES PREFER TO HAVE BIGGER FAMILIES?

Often the reason is necessity. In poorer countries, for example in Asia and Africa, life expectancy is low. Many children die young. People may choose to have more children, to make sure enough survive to work and support the rest of the family as they grow older.

This family live in Mali, a country in West Africa.

Some governments encourage people to have smaller families. This places less demand on resources, such as food and fuel for energy.

CHINA HAS TRIED TO LIMIT ITS FAMILY SIZE FOR MORE THAN 30 YEARS

DATE	GOVERNMENT ACTION
1962	GOVERNMENT REALISES POPULATION IS GROWING TOO FAST.
1970s	ADVISES FEWER BIRTHS AND LONGER GAPS BETWEEN HAVING CHILDREN. PUSHES POLICY OF 'ONE CHILD IS BEST, TWO AT MOST'.
1980	ONE-CHILD POLICY INTRODUCED. SINGLE-PARENT FAMILIES 'REWARDED' WITH FREE EDUCATION, HOUSING BENEFITS AND TV AND VIDEO. REWARDS TAKEN AWAY IF SECOND CHILD BORN.
1988	ONE-CHILD POLICY SCRAPPED, AS UNPOPULAR. FARMING COMMUNITIES NEED LARGE FAMILIES TO WORK IN FIELDS. NOW ALLOWED SECOND CHILD, OR THIRD IF FIRST TWO ARE GIRLS.

Connect!

WHAT HAPPENS WHEN FAMILIES BREAK DOWN? CHECK OUT Q22.

ADOPTION THIS IS WHEN CHILDREN ARE TAKEN INTO FAMILIES BY PEOPLE WHO ARE NOT ACTUALLY THEIR NATURAL PARENTS. THE CHILDREN BECOME PART OF THEIR NEW FAMILIES.

☆ WHAT IS A FAMILY TREE?

IT IS A CHART WHICH SHOWS HOW EVERYONE IS RELATED IN A FAMILY. EACH LEVEL OF THE FAMILY TREE REPRESENTS A DIFFERENT GENERATION.

HOW MANY OF THESE FAMILY MEMBERS DO YOU HAVE?

NEPHEW = YOUR BROTHER/SISTER'S MALE CHILD.
NIECE = YOUR BROTHER/SISTER'S FEMALE CHILD.
SISTER-IN-LAW = YOUR BROTHER'S WIFE.
BROTHER-IN-LAW = YOUR SISTER'S HUSBAND.
AUNT = EITHER OF YOUR PARENT'S SISTER.
UNCLE = EITHER OF YOUR PARENT'S BROTHER.
COUSIN = THE CHILD OF THE BROTHER/SISTER OF EITHER PARENT.
GRANDPARENTS = EITHER OF YOUR PARENT'S PARENTS.

Connect!

TURN TO Q36 TO SEE HOW QUICKLY THE WORLD'S POPULATION IS GROWING.

☆NOT ALL FATHERS ARE MALE! IN THE AFRICAN **NUER TRIBE**, A CHILD AND ITS MOTHER LIVE WITH ANOTHER WOMAN.

18 What is marriage?

A marriage is a legal agreement between a man and a woman to live together as husband and wife. When they marry, some people prefer a simple civil ceremony, while others choose to follow a religious or traditional ceremony.

The Christian wedding

☆ **TRADITIONS**

IN CHRISTIAN COUNTRIES, IT IS TRADITIONAL TO GET MARRIED IN A CHURCH. THE BRIDE WEARS A **WHITE DRESS**, WHICH INDICATES PURITY. THE **VEIL** IS BELIEVED TO REFLECT AWAY ANY BAD LUCK. THE **RING** IS A SYMBOL OF LOVE TO BIND THE COUPLE TOGETHER. IT IS WORN ON THE BRIDE'S FOURTH FINGER OF THE LEFT HAND, BECAUSE IT WAS ONCE BELIEVED A VEIN RAN FROM THIS FINGER TO THE HEART (ANOTHER SYMBOL OF LOVE). THE **BANNS** ARE ANNOUNCEMENTS MADE IN THE CHURCH SEVERAL WEEKS BEFORE THE MARRIAGE, TO TELL PEOPLE THAT THE WEDDING IS HAPPENING.

The Jewish wedding

☆ **TRADITIONS**

JEWISH WEDDINGS TRADITIONALLY TAKE PLACE INSIDE A SYNAGOGUE. ONE PART OF THE MARRIAGE CEREMONY INVOLVES THE BRIDEGROOM **STEPPING ON A GLASS DRINKING VESSEL**. THIS SYMBOLISES THE FRAGILE NATURE OF LOVE AND HOW EASILY IT CAN BE DESTROYED.

The Hindu wedding

☆ **TRADITIONS**

AT HINDU WEDDINGS, THE BRIDE'S FACE IS DECORATED WITH MAKE-UP AND JEWELLERY. AN IMPORTANT RITUAL IS THE **SAATH-PERE**. THIS INVOLVES WALKING ROUND A SACRED FIRE SEVEN TIMES. THE COUPLE ARE TIED BY A PIECE OF CLOTH TO SHOW THEIR BOND.

The Chinese wedding

☆ **TRADITIONS**

CHINESE BRIDES TRADITIONALLY DRESS IN **RED**. BEFORE THE CEREMONY ITSELF, THE BRIDE IS CARRIED FROM HER HOUSE TO THE WEDDING IN A COVERED SEDAN CHAIR, TO SHELTER HER FROM EVIL INFLUENCES.

MARRIAGE MILESTONES

THE OLDEST COUPLE = HARRY STEVE (103) AND THELMA LUCAS (84), FROM WISCONSIN, USA.
THE YOUNGEST COUPLE = IN 1986, AN 11-MONTH-OLD BOY FROM BANGLADESH, WAS MARRIED TO A 3-MONTH-OLD GIRL.
THE MOST EXPENSIVE WEDDING = THE WEDDING OF DUBAI'S PRINCESS SALAMA IN 1981 COST £22 MILLION.
THE BIGGEST MASS WEDDING CEREMONY = THIS TOOK PLACE ON 25 AUGUST 1992 IN SEOUL, SOUTH KOREA. 20,825 COUPLES WERE MARRIED AT THE SAME TIME, WITH A FURTHER 9,800 COUPLES TAKING PART BY SATELLITE. →

Connect!

WHAT IS LOVE AND WHY DO WE FEEL IT? CHECK OUT Q24.

19 What is an arranged marriage?

This is a marriage where parents choose the partners for their children.

Muslim, Hindu and Sikh parents may insist that they select their children's marriage partner. The Tiwi people of the Australian island of Melville arrange a girl's marriage before she is even born.

QUESTION 20 Is there anyone you can't marry?

Yes. Here are some examples.

ROMAN CATHOLIC PRIESTS, THE POPE, NUNS AND MONKS They are forbidden to marry so that they can devote their life completely to God and the Church.

UNDER-AGED PARTNERS In Britain and most of the USA, both partners must be at least 18. This is the age the law recognises them as adults. They can marry when 16, but only if their parents agree.

CLOSE FAMILY MEMBERS Marriage between cousins is legal, but not between any closer relatives. One reason is because children born from a closer partnership run the risk of inheriting a genetic disease.

WHAT ABOUT GAY PEOPLE?

Gay, or homosexual, people are attracted to members of the same sex. Some countries, including Denmark, Greenland, the Netherlands, Norway, Sweden, Spain and parts of the United States, have passed 'partnership laws'. Under these laws, partners have the same legal rights as a married couple, but they cannot have a church marriage, or adopt a child. At least one of the two people must be a citizen of that country.

QUESTION 21 Can you be married to more than one person at a time?

Yes, some people can.

In most societies, people marry just one person at a time. This is called **monogamy**. But in places such as the Middle East and Central Africa, people sometimes have several partners at once. This is known as **polygamy**. A Muslim can have up to four wives, but only if each is treated equally.

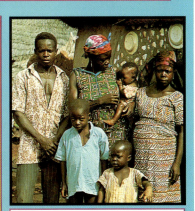

↑ This farmer, who lives in Ghana, in West Africa, has two wives.

QUESTION 22 What happens when a marriage breaks down?

The formal parting of two married people is called a divorce.

Sometimes, people find they are no longer happy together. They separate and solicitors may eventually draw a legal end to their marriage. When the couple divorce, a court may decide how their joint belongings are to be split, and who will look after any children. Or the couple may decide themselves.

WHEN EDWARD VIII FELL IN LOVE WITH WALLIS SIMPSON, SOCIETY WAS SHOCKED, BECAUSE SHE WAS DIVORCED. HE WANTED TO MARRY WALLIS, BUT THE GOVERNMENT DID NOT BELIEVE THE BRITISH PEOPLE WOULD APPROVE OF HER. EDWARD WENT THROUGH WITH THE MARRIAGE, BUT AS A RESULT WAS FORCED TO GIVE UP THE THRONE.

GETTING DIVORCED FROM HIS WIFE IVANA COST DONALD TRUMP, AN AMERICAN PROPERTY TYCOON, £11 MILLION!

Connect!

HOW DOES BEING IN THE PUBLIC EYE AFFECT HOW PEOPLE VIEW YOU? SEE Q25.

QUESTION

23 What are feelings?

A feeling is an emotional response to a particular situation, person or event.

WHAT IS SYMPATHY?

To be sympathetic to another person is to share the same emotion, or feeling, as that person.

WE MAY FEEL

LOVE

FEAR

DISGUST

SURPRISE

PRIDE

Connect!

TURN TO Q46 TO SEE WHAT CAN HAPPEN WHEN MANY PEOPLE FEEL A STRONG EMOTION ABOUT AN ISSUE.

QUESTION

24 What is love?

Love is a very strong feeling or deep affection for a person or thing.

☆ WHAT HAPPENS IN THE BODY?

Scientists have identified several chemicals released by the body when we fall in love. One of them is phenylethylamine (PEA). It seems to stimulate the brain and evokes feelings of happiness and comfort. PEA is also found in cocoa, which may be why people are so fond of chocolate.

Prove It!

When we are attracted to someone, our pupils grow bigger. See whether a friend's pupils grow wide when showing them pictures of their favourite pop or film star.

☆ HOW DO WE BEHAVE?

OUR LEGS GO WEAK.

THE HEART BEATS FASTER.

OUR BREATHING SPEEDS UP.

THE PUPILS OF THE EYES EXPAND.

BLOOD RUSHES TO THE SURFACE OF THE SKIN.

QUESTION

25 Why do we remember people long after they have died?

Some people make such an impact on the world that they are worshipped or admired for many years.

1 FAMOUS FOR...
WHAT THEY ACHIEVED WHILE THEY WERE ALIVE

MARIE CURIE (1867–1934) SHE WAS A POLISH SCIENTIST WHO PIONEERED WORK ON RADIATION. SHE ENRICHED PEOPLE'S SCIENTIFIC KNOWLEDGE.

2 FAMOUS FOR...
AFFECTING THE WAY PEOPLE LIVE TOGETHER ON EARTH

MARTIN LUTHER KING (1929–1968) HE WAS A CIVIL RIGHTS LEADER IN THE 1950s AND 1960s, WHO HELPED BLACK PEOPLE IN THE USA ACHIEVE CIVIL RIGHTS.

26

What makes us laugh?

Everyone's sense of humour is unique. It is healthy to laugh.

- WHEN YOU HAVE A CHUCKLE YOU EXERCISE ALL THE BODY'S MUSCLE GROUPS.
- A TEN-SECOND LAUGH RAISES THE HEART RATE TO THE SAME LEVEL AS A TEN-MINUTE ROWING SESSION.

THERE ARE MANY DIFFERENT TYPES OF COMEDY, HERE ARE JUST A FEW...	
IRONY	SAYING ONE THING, MEANING THE OPPOSITE.
FARCE, SLAPSTICK	VISUAL, PLAYFUL HUMOUR, LIKE CUSTARD-PIE THROWING.
MIMICRY	COPYING OTHER PEOPLE'S HABITS AND SPEECH.

QUESTION

27

What makes us cry?

If we feel sad or emotional, we may shed tears.

What happens when we cry? Our eyes are constantly making tears to keep the eyeballs moist. When we cry, the tear glands produce more water than normal. Some is carried away by tear ducts, some falls as tears, and the rest floods into a tube that links the eyes to the nose.

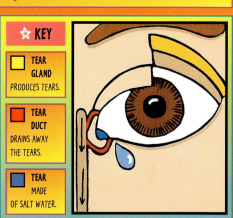

★ KEY

- **TEAR GLAND** PRODUCES TEARS.
- **TEAR DUCT** DRAINS AWAY THE TEARS.
- **TEAR** MADE OF SALT WATER.

☆ HUMANS ARE THE ONLY ANIMALS THAT CRY BECAUSE OF EMOTION!

What is obsession?

Sometimes hero worship can lead to a person being preoccupied by – sometimes even haunted by – their hero. This is called obsession.

ELVIS PRESLEY (1935–1977) HE WAS ONE OF THE MOST POPULAR AMERICAN SINGERS IN THE HISTORY OF ROCK MUSIC.

ELVIS LOOKALIKE TODAY, NEARLY TWENTY YEARS AFTER HIS DEATH, PEOPLE ARE STILL FASCINATED BY THE LIFE, LOOK AND MUSIC OF ELVIS.

3 FAMOUS FOR... THEIR MIRACULOUS POWERS AND TEACHINGS

JESUS CHRIST HE WAS A JEW LIVING 2000 YEARS AGO. CHRISTIANS BELIEVE HE IS THE SON OF GOD. HIS LIFE AND REPORTED MIRACLES ARE DESCRIBED IN THE BIBLE.

4 FAMOUS FOR... SYMBOLISING THE TIME, OR ERA, IN WHICH THEY LIVED

JAMES DEAN (1931–1955) HE WAS AN AMERICAN MOVIE STAR WHO WAS KILLED IN A CAR CRASH WHEN HE WAS 24. HE IS STILL REMEMBERED AS A YOUTH ICON.

QUESTION

28

What makes us scared?

Fear is a survival reaction.

THE BODY REACTS TO FEAR IN A NUMBER OF WAYS, MAKING US READY TO EITHER 'FIGHT' OR 'FLEE' THE OBJECT CAUSING THE FEAR.

1 SKIN MAY TURN PALER – BLOOD GOES TO OTHER PARTS OF THE BODY WHERE IT IS NEEDED MORE.

2 HEART BEATS FASTER, PUMPING MORE BLOOD TO MUSCLES AND BRAIN.

3 BREATHING SPEEDS UP, FLOODING BLOOD WITH OXYGEN.

4 HAIR STANDS UP, MAKING US LOOK 'BIGGER'.

★ PHOBIAS

A PHOBIA IS AN UNREASONABLE FEAR, USUALLY LINKED TO ONE SPECIFIC CIRCUMSTANCE OR EXPERIENCE.

CLAUSTROPHOBIA = FEAR OF CLOSED SPACES.
TRISKEDEPHOBIA = FEAR OF THE NUMBER 13.
XENOPHOBIA = FEAR OF FOREIGN PEOPLE.
SCOPOPHOBIA = FEAR OF BEING STARED AT.
DORAPHOBIA = FEAR OF FUR.
PHOBOPHOBIA = FEAR OF FEAR ITSELF.

Connect!

CAN YOU BE BORN POWERFUL OR FAMOUS? TO FIND OUT TURN TO Q30.

Connect!

WHAT HAPPENS WHEN FEAR LEADS TO PREJUDICE? TURN TO Q46 TO FIND OUT.

QUESTION

29 Why are some people more powerful than others?

Power means influence or authority. Some people have such great power that it affects the world and those who live in it. What makes people powerful?

Money

When money is no object, a person has freedom to make almost any decision they choose: where and how they live, what they buy, where they can travel and so on.

⬆ The Sultan of Brunei is the world's richest man. He has an estimated fortune of nearly $40,000 million.

Position

Heads of government, such as Prime Ministers and Presidents, have the huge responsibility of making decisions that affect the people of their country.

NAME: BILL CLINTON.
POSITION: PRESIDENT OF THE USA FROM 1992.
RESPONSIBLE FOR: POPULATION OF NEARLY 240 MILLION.
TYPICAL DUTIES: THE HEAD OF LAW ENFORCEMENT FOR THE NATIONAL GOVERNMENT; COMMANDER IN CHIEF OF THE ARMY AND NAVY; APPOINTS AMBASSADORS, MINISTERS AND JUDGES; MAKES TREATIES WITH SUPPORT OF SENATE.

Influence

Karol Wojtyla has influence over more than 1,000 million people, because he is also known as Pope John Paul II. As the current head of the Roman Catholic Church, he is seen as God's representative on Earth. So, nearly one-sixth of the world's population observe his teachings.

POWER CAN COME WITH A PRICE. IN NOVEMBER 1963, PRESIDENT JOHN KENNEDY BECAME THE FOURTH US PRESIDENT TO BE KILLED IN OFFICE.

Power can endanger lives. On 15 February 1989, Iran's religious leader Ayatollah Khomeini placed a fatwa, or death warrant, on author Salman Rushdie. The Ayatollah was angered by the writer's book, 'The Satanic Verses', believing it insulted the religion of Islam.

Connect!

FIND OUT HOW THE WORLD IS RUN IN Q44.

QUESTION

30 Can you be born powerful?

Yes, you can inherit power. Wealth and position can be passed from one generation to another.

MEMBERS OF THE WALTON FAMILY, IN THE USA, ARE AMONG **THE RICHEST PEOPLE IN THE WORLD**. THEIR RETAIL BUSINESS IS WORTH AN ESTIMATED $24,000 MILLION. CHILDREN IN THE FAMILY INHERIT THE BUSINESS AND THE WEALTH.

IN 1937, A BOY CALLED TENZIN GYATSO, FROM TIBET, WAS VISITED BY A GROUP OF BUDDHIST HOLY MEN. HE GAVE ANSWERS TO QUESTIONS THAT ONLY THE DALAI LAMA WOULD KNOW, AND THEY HAILED THE 2-YEAR-OLD AS THE NEW **DALAI LAMA** – THE LEADER OF THE TIBETAN PEOPLE. BUDDHISTS THINK PEOPLE ARE RE-BORN AFTER THEY DIE, SO TENZIN IS BELIEVED TO BE THE OLD DALAI LAMA IN A NEW BODY.

DURING THE RUSSIAN REVOLUTION IN 1917, TSAR NICHOLAS II WAS FORCED TO GIVE UP HIS THRONE. MANY PEOPLE WERE POOR AND UNHAPPY, AND WANTED 'BREAD, PEACE AND LAND'.

31 Can power make people corrupt?

Power is about making your will felt. Some people increase their power by controlling and terrifying others.

Gangsters

Dictators

Al Capone became rich and famous through his activities during America's Prohibition period (1920-33). This banned the sale and manufacture of alcohol. Capone and fellow gangsters achieved power by setting up illegal drinking dens.

THE MAFIA is a secret organisation that started in Sicily, Italy, in the 13th century. Members carry out illegal activities, such as selling drugs and demanding protection money from people. They are powerful because people are frightened to give evidence against them. Those who report the Mafia to the police are often hurt or even murdered.

A dictator is someone who rules with supreme and often dangerous authority.

CASE STUDY WORLD WAR II (1939-1945)

German dictator Adolf Hitler came to power in 1933. As leader of the Nazi party, he blamed Germany's economic problems on the Jewish people, and other minorities, such as gypsies and gay people. Up to 26 million people were killed in concentration camps. The German army tried to reclaim land it had lost in World War I. Among other countries, it invaded Poland, France, Norway and Belgium.

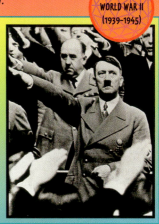

32 How can people use their power to make the world a better place?

CASE STUDY NELSON MANDELA

Political and religious leaders can use their influence to improve our world.

Connect! WHY DO WARS HAPPEN? TURN TO Q41.

Connect! HOW PEOPLE LIVE IN THEIR COUNTRY DEPENDS ON MORE THAN POLITICS. SEE Q43.

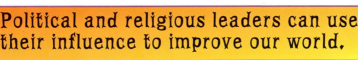

NAME NELSON ROLIHLAHLA MANDELA.

HISTORY MANDELA WAS BORN IN 1918. HE WORKED AS A SOUTH AFRICAN LAWYER AND BECAME THE LEADER OF THE AFRICAN NATIONAL CONGRESS (ANC). HE WAS ARRESTED IN 1962, AND SENTENCED TO LIFE IMPRISONMENT IN 1964, FOR HIS BELIEF THAT SOUTH AFRICA SHOULD BE A FREE, DEMOCRATIC SOCIETY, WITH ALL RACES LIVING HARMONIOUSLY TOGETHER. HE WAS FINALLY RELEASED IN 1989. HIS CAMPAIGN TO ABOLISH THE POLICY OF RACIAL DISCRIMINATION AND SEPARATION IN SOUTH AFRICA (APARTHEID) HAD BEEN SUCCESSFUL.

POSITION IN JUNE 1994, NELSON MANDELA WAS ELECTED AS PRESIDENT OF SOUTH AFRICA.

AT THE TIME OF HIS TRIAL IN 1964, MANDELA SAID: **I HAVE CHERISHED THE IDEAL OF A DEMOCRATIC AND FREE SOCIETY IN WHICH ALL PERSONS LIVE TOGETHER IN HARMONY. IT IS AN IDEAL WHICH I HOPE TO LIVE FOR AND ACHIEVE. BUT IF NEEDS BE IT IS AN IDEAL FOR WHICH I AM PREPARED TO DIE.**

☆ SOUTH AFRICA IN 1964

- A MINORITY WHITE GOVERNMENT IN POWER, EVEN THOUGH MAJORITY OF POPULATION (87%) IS BLACK.
- SYSTEM OF APARTHEID, WHICH DISCRIMINATED AGAINST PEOPLE BECAUSE OF THEIR RACE, KEPT BLACK PEOPLE APART FROM WHITES.
- BLACK PEOPLE WERE NOT ALLOWED TO VOTE IN ELECTIONS, SO HAD FEW RIGHTS.

NOTICE DELIVERY BOYS AND AFRICAN SERVANTS ENTRANCE IN LANE

WHITES WAITING ROOM BLANKE WAGKAMER

☆ SOUTH AFRICA TODAY

- A MAJORITY BLACK GOVERNMENT IN POWER, LED BY NELSON MANDELA.
- APARTHEID ABOLISHED.
- BLACK PEOPLE VOTED FOR FIRST TIME IN 1994.

QUESTION

33

How do people get their message across?

We use a combination of spoken and written languages to tell each other how we feel and what we believe.

☆ WHAT IS LANGUAGE?

The word language comes from the Latin word, 'lingua', meaning tongue. Spoken languages have three things in common:

A SOUND-PATTERN = THE SOUNDS THAT THE HUMAN SPEECH ORGANS CAN MAKE.
WORDS = SOUND-PATTERNS THAT HAVE A MEANING, REPRESENTING OBJECTS, ACTIONS OR IDEAS.
GRAMMATICAL STRUCTURE = THE COMBINATION OF WORDS INTO SENTENCES.

☆ WHO INVENTED LANGUAGE?

No-one really knows how language began. It probably developed slowly from the grunts and groans of early cavemen. As human brains and vocal equipment became bigger, so did the ability to talk. The first written evidence that language existed was the discovery of Sumerian word-pictures made about 3500BC and Egyptian hieroglyphics, dating from about 3000BC.

HOW DO WE LEARN TO SPEAK?

YOUNG CHILDREN INSTINCTIVELY WANT TO COMMUNICATE HOW THEY FEEL, SO THEY LISTEN TO THE SOUNDS AROUND THEM AND THEN START TO IMITATE THEM. THEY GRADUALLY LEARN TO SELECT THE SOUNDS THAT MAKE UP WORDS AND DISREGARD THE REST.

THERE'S MORE TO COMMUNICATION THAN JUST SPEAKING. PEOPLE CONVEY A LOT OF INFORMATION IN THEIR GESTURES. THIS IS CALLED **BODY LANGUAGE**. **LIE DETECTORS** ARE MACHINES WHICH TRY TO DECIDE WHETHER WE ARE TELLING THE TRUTH. THEY WORK BY MONITORING VARIOUS PHYSICAL CHANGES IN RESPONSE TO QUESTIONS. THESE INCLUDE BLOOD PRESSURE, PULSE RATE AND LEVELS OF PERSPIRATION.

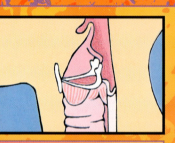

How do we use our mouths to speak?

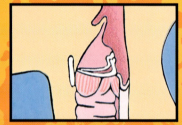

SPEECH IS PRODUCED MAINLY BY THE ACTIONS OF THE VOCAL CORDS. THESE ARE SMALL BANDS OF TISSUE STRETCHING ACROSS THE VOICE-BOX, OR LARYNX.

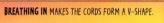

BREATHING IN MAKES THE CORDS FORM A V-SHAPE.

BREATHING OUT AND SPEAKING CAUSES MUSCLES TO NARROW THE CORDS. AIR VIBRATES THE TIGHTENED CORDS AND PRODUCES SOUND.

QUESTION

34

Why don't we all speak the same language?

There are around 3,000 languages spoken in the world today, not including dialects, which are local variations on a common language.

Prove It!

See if you can translate the following Esperanto sentence:
La astronauto, per speciala instrumento, fotografa la lunon.

The many different languages spoken in the world today developed slowly from a few earlier or core languages. People became divided into groups and settled in various parts of the world. With little contact between the groups, the languages gradually became more and more different. After a number of centuries, they had become so distinct that the groups could no longer understand each other.

LANGUAGE	NUMBER OF SPEAKERS
MANDARIN CHINESE	825 MILLION
ENGLISH	431 MILLION
HINDI	325 MILLION
SPANISH	320 MILLION
RUSSIAN	289 MILLION
ARABIC	187 MILLION
BENGALI	178 MILLION
PORTUGUESE	169 MILLION
MALAY-INDONESIAN	135 MILLION
JAPANESE	124 MILLION

☆ MISSING SOUNDS

NOT ALL LANGUAGES HAVE THE SAME SOUNDS

PUNJABI	HAS NO **V** SOUND.
CHINESE	HAS NO **L** OR **R** SOUNDS.
GERMAN	HAS **CH** SOUND WHICH IS DIFFICULT FOR ENGLISH SPEAKERS.
FRENCH	ROLL THE **R** SOUND AND HAVE DIFFICULTY WITH **TH** SOUND ('THIS' BECOMES 'ZIS').
SWAHILI	USES MANY WHISTLES AND CLICKS OF THE TONGUE.

☆ COULD WE ALL SPEAK A COMMON LANGUAGE?

OVER THE YEARS, AT LEAST 600 COMMON LANGUAGES HAVE BEEN SUGGESTED.

ESPERANTO IS THE MOST SUCCESSFUL. IT WAS INVENTED IN 1887, AND IS SPOKEN BY AROUND 10 MILLION PEOPLE IN OVER 90 COUNTRIES.

☆ THE ANSWER TO THE **PROVE IT!** IS 'THE ASTRONAUT, WITH A SPECIAL INSTRUMENT, PHOTOGRAPHS THE MOON'.

The

world

is full of them...

people

Where's the most crowded place on Earth?

 # Who rules the world?

Why don't people stay in one place?

To find out how people live on
Earth, turn the page and read
PART THREE.----➤

QUESTION 35

How many people are there in the world?

In 1994, there were around 5,666 million people on the globe.

QUESTION 36

How quickly is the world's population increasing?

Very fast indeed! Examine these facts.

☆ INCREASE SINCE THE FIRST PEOPLE

Since the first people inhabited the planet, it has taken nearly the whole of human history for the population to reach 1,000 million. It then took just another 80 years for the population to double. A major cause for this sudden increase was the start of the Industrial Revolution – it gave people jobs, roofs over their heads, money to buy food, and access to medicine.

YEAR	MILLIONS OF PEOPLE IN THE WORLD
2000BC	108
1000BC	120
AD 1	138
AD 1000	275
AD 2000	6,251 (estimate)

☆ INCREASE IN THE 20TH CENTURY

YEAR	MILLIONS OF PEOPLE IN THE WORLD
1900	1,633
1920	1,862
1940	2,295
1960	3,019
1980	4,450
2000	6,251 (estimate)
2050	11,600 (estimate)

THE WORLD IS ADDING THE EQUIVALENT OF:
- ONE CHINA'S-WORTH OF PEOPLE EVERY TEN YEARS
- ONE MEXICO'S-WORTH EVERY YEAR
- ONE NEW YORK CITY'S-WORTH EVERY MONTH

Prove It!

At the present rate, world population is doubling every 40 years. Check this on the chart.

Connect!

FIND OUT IN Q38 HOW OVERPOPULATION CAN CAUSE PROBLEMS.

TOTAL POPULATION INCREASE PER MINUTE = 178

QUESTION 37

Where is the most crowded place?

The population of the world is unevenly distributed. Almost three-quarters of people live in just two continents – Asia and Europe.

POPULATION DENSITY
AVERAGE NUMBER OF PEOPLE PER SQ KM:
ASIA = 73
EUROPE = 66
AFRICA = 22
N AMERICA = 18
S AMERICA = 17
AUSTRALIA = 2
ANTARCTICA = NO PERMANENT POPULATION

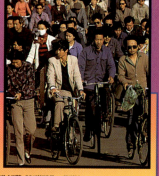

MOST POPULATED COUNTRY = CHINA:
CHINA'S POPULATION IS 1,166 MILLION.
INDIA (CURRENTLY 890 MILLION) IS EXPECTED TO OVERTAKE CHINA IN THE YEAR 2050, WITH A PREDICTED 1,591 MILLION PEOPLE AGAINST CHINA'S 1,555 MILLION.

☆ IN 1959, A HOUSE IN HONG KONG DESIGNED FOR 12 PEOPLE WAS FOUND TO CONTAIN 459 OCCUPANTS – INCLUDING FOUR ON THE ROOF.

38 Can the planet support all these people?

More and more people are making demands on the Earth, and its valuable resources are being used up. The planet faces serious problems.

FOOD = ENOUGH FOOD IS GROWN TO FEED EVERYONE, BUT RESOURCES ARE CONCENTRATED IN THE DEVELOPED WORLD, WHILE DEVELOPING COUNTRIES ARE OFTEN POOR AND HUNGRY.

POLLUTION = CAUSES GLOBAL WARMING AND DAMAGES THE OZONE LAYER, WHICH PROTECTS US FROM THE SUN'S HARMFUL RAYS.

UNEMPLOYMENT = NOT ENOUGH JOBS FOR EVERYONE, RESULTING IN DISSATISFACTION, INCREASED CRIME AND SOCIAL UNREST.

FUEL = OIL, GAS AND COAL SUPPLIES ARE RUNNING OUT.

Connect! WHEN PEOPLE GET WORRIED ABOUT PROTECTING THEIR RESOURCES, WARS BREAK OUT. SEE Q41.

---

39 Why don't people stay in one place?

Advances in technology and communication have made it easier for people that can afford to travel to do so.

Before the 15th century, most people did not move away from the country of their birth. It was too difficult to negotiate mountain ranges, ocean expanses and deserts. In some of the developing world, this is still the case.

☆ WHY DO PEOPLE MOVE?

- BETTER JOB PROSPECTS.
- NEW LAND FOR FARMING.
- ESCAPE FROM PERSECUTION.
- FLEEING FROM NATURAL DISASTERS, SUCH AS FAMINE OR PLAGUES.
- FLEEING FROM MAN-MADE DISASTERS, SUCH AS WAR.

☆ WHAT ARE THE EFFECTS OF IMMIGRATION?

PROS = COUNTRY RECEIVING IMMIGRANTS BENEFITS FROM THEIR CUSTOMS, FOOD AND CULTURE. A MULTICULTURAL SOCIETY EDUCATES LOCAL PEOPLE INTO UNDERSTANDING DIFFERENT RACES.

CONS = ACCEPTING COUNTRY MAY NOT HAVE ENOUGH JOBS. 'BRAIN DRAIN' CAN OCCUR – THOUSANDS OF EUROPEAN SCIENTISTS HAVE EMIGRATED TO AUSTRALIA AND THE USA IN THE HOPE OF BETTER JOB OPPORTUNITIES.

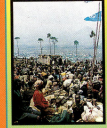

NOT ALL MOVEMENT HAPPENS VOLUNTARILY. OVER 14 MILLION MIGRANTS ARE **REFUGEES** – PEOPLE WHO ARE FLEEING A WAR, PERSECUTION OR A NATURAL DISASTER. THESE RWANDAN REFUGEES ARE ESCAPING FROM A CIVIL WAR.

---

40 How is the world map changing?

There have been many changes to the world map this century.

1 Some countries have changed their names: Rhodesia to Zimbabwe, Ceylon to Sri Lanka, Upper Volta to Burkina Faso and Persia to Iran.

2 The Partition of India in 1947 created the separate state of Pakistan.

3 The USSR disappeared in 1992, and was replaced by the Commonwealth of Independent States.

4 The Berlin Wall came down in November 1989 and Germany was no longer divided.

GERMANY IS UNITED, AS THE BERLIN WALL IS TAKEN DOWN.

☆ WHERE DOES MOST MIGRATION OCCUR?

AN **IMMIGRANT** IS SOMEONE WHO HAS SETTLED IN A FOREIGN COUNTRY. AN **EMIGRANT** LEAVES HIS OWN COUNTRY FOR ANOTHER.

IMMIGRATION THE UNITED STATES RECEIVES THE MOST IMMIGRANTS. NEARLY 60 MILLION PEOPLE ARRIVED BETWEEN 1820 AND 1991.

EMIGRATION MORE PEOPLE ARE QUEUEING UP TO LEAVE MEXICO THAN ANY OTHER COUNTRY IN THE WORLD.

Connect! WHY ARE SOME COUNTRIES RICH AND OTHERS POOR? SEE Q43.

QUESTION

41 What are wars?

Wars are large-scale attacks waged between countries or groups of people. They are fought to gain power over land, money, resources and other people.

Zulu Wars
(1838-1879)

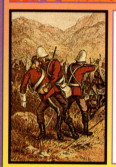

IN THE 19TH CENTURY, WHITE SETTLERS TRIED TO CONQUER AFRICA TO TURN IT INTO EUROPEAN COLONIES. THE ZULU NATIVES IN SOUTH AFRICA DID NOT WANT TO GIVE UP THEIR LAND. THEY FOUGHT MANY FIERCE BATTLES, BUT WERE FINALLY DEFEATED BY THE BRITISH.

Vietnam War
(1965-1975)

IN THE EARLY 1960s, US TROOPS WERE SENT TO VIETNAM, IN SOUTH-EAST ASIA. THEY WERE THERE TO HELP DEFEND SOUTH VIETNAM FROM THE NORTH. THE NORTHERN GOVERNMENT WANTED TO REUNITE AND CONTROL THE DIVIDED COUNTRY. MORE THAN TWO MILLION SOUTH VIETNAMESE AND ALMOST 50,000 AMERICAN SOLDIERS DIED.

Gulf War
(1990-1991)

IRAQ INVADED KUWAIT, UNDER THE INSTRUCTIONS OF DICTATOR SADDAM HUSSEIN. HE BELIEVED KUWAIT WAS REALLY PART OF IRAQ. CONQUERING KUWAIT WOULD ALSO HAVE GIVEN IRAQ BETTER ACCESS TO THE VALUABLE SHIPPING LANES OF THE GULF. BUT BRITISH AND AMERICAN TROOPS MANAGED TO FORCE THE IRAQI ARMY OUT.

Connect!

WHAT IS DEMOCRACY? SEE Q45.

☆ HAVE THERE ALWAYS BEEN WARS?

There are many records of ancient battles between nations. When the Greeks and Persians fought in 479BC at Plataea, it was reported that 250,000 people lost their lives. In AD 451, in a battle between the Huns and the Romans at Châlons-sur Marne, in France, legend has it that 200,000 soldiers were killed in a single day.

THE EARLIEST SURVIVING WEAPON IS A WOODEN SPEAR FOUND IN APRIL 1911 AT CLACTON-ON-SEA, ESSEX, IN ENGLAND. IT HAS BEEN ESTIMATED THAT IT WAS MADE BEFORE 200,000BC.

HOW LONG DO WARS LAST?

THE SHORTEST WAR WAS THE ONE BETWEEN BRITAIN AND ZANZIBAR, WHICH IS NOW PART OF TANZANIA. THIS WAR LASTED FROM 9.02AM TO 9.40AM ON 27 AUGUST 1896. AFTER ATTACKING THE PALACE FOR 38 MINUTES THE SELF-APPOINTED SULTAN SA'ID KHALID SURRENDERED TO REAR-ADMIRAL HARRY RAWSON AND HIS ARMY.

THE LONGEST CONTINUOUS WAR WAS THE THIRTY YEARS WAR BETWEEN VARIOUS EUROPEAN COUNTRIES FROM 1618 TO 1648. THE MAP OF EUROPE WAS DRAMATICALLY ALTERED AS A RESULT OF THIS CONFLICT.

☆ WHAT IS A CONSCIENTIOUS OBJECTOR?

A person who feels that his conscience will not let him carry out his required duties is called a conscientious objector. In World War II, the British soldier Gilbert Lane was court-martialled six times for refusing to fight. He served 31 months' detention and 183 days' imprisonment.

QUESTION

42 What effect do wars have on the population of the world?

Study these facts.

1 THE BLOODIEST BATTLE FOUGHT IN BRITAIN IS THOUGHT TO HAVE BEEN THE BATTLE OF TOWTON, NEAR TADCASTER, NORTH YORKSHIRE, DURING THE WARS OF THE ROSES. ON 29 MARCH 1461, 36,000 YORKISTS DEFEATED 40,000 LANCASTRIANS. BETWEEN 28,000 AND 38,000 PEOPLE LOST THEIR LIVES.

2 IN THE PARAGUAYAN WAR OF 1864-70, AGAINST BRAZIL, ARGENTINA AND URUGUAY, PARAGUAY'S POPULATION WAS REDUCED FROM 1,400,000 TO 220,000. ONLY 30,000 OF THESE WERE ADULT MALES.

3 IT IS ESTIMATED THAT 54.8 MILLION SOLDIERS AND CIVILIANS LOST THEIR LIVES IN WORLD WAR II (1939-45). THIS IS THE MOST NUMBER OF PEOPLE TO HAVE PERISHED IN A SINGLE WAR. 25 MILLION SOVIET PEOPLE DIED AND 7.8 MILLION CHINESE CIVILIANS. POLAND LOST 17.2% OF ITS POPULATION.

43 Why are some countries rich and some poor?

A nation's wealth is linked to its people, resources and capital.

If people are healthy, skilled and educated they can produce much more. A country may have resources, but no means of using them. The money to build roads and factories, and acquire technology to use resources is called capital.

A COUNTRY'S TRADE DEPENDS ON THE GOODS THAT IT EXPORTS AND IMPORTS.

EXPORTING = SELLING GOODS TO OTHER COUNTRIES.
IMPORTING = BUYING IN GOODS FROM OTHER COUNTRIES.

TO TRADE SUCCESSFULLY, COUNTRIES NEED TO HAVE GOOD TRANSPORT LINKS NATIONWIDE AND WORLDWIDE. THEY ALSO NEED TO PRODUCE, AND SUPPLY, GOODS WHICH ARE IN DEMAND.

↑ Goods passing through a container port in Nigeria.

Prove It!

Can you guess what the biggest exports of Australia, India and Japan are? The answers are hidden on this page.

ONLY 500 YEARS AGO PARTS OF AFRICA, INDIA AND CHINA WERE MORE TECHNOLOGICALLY ADVANCED THAN EUROPE. THESE COUNTRIES WERE COLONISED BY EUROPEANS, WHO TOOK THEIR WEALTH AND TECHNOLOGY TO SET UP THEIR OWN INDUSTRIES.

Connect!

TURN TO Q47 TO SEE HOW DIFFERENT RACES LEARN TO LIVE IN THEIR ENVIRONMENT.

CASE STUDY SAUDI ARABIA

Countries in the Middle East are among the richest in the world. Their wealth comes from exporting oil. The fuel is valuable because it can only be drilled in a few places. Saudi Arabia produces over 8,000 million barrels of oil each day.

CASE STUDY NAURU

The tiny republic of Nauru, in the Pacific Ocean, has become rich by exporting fertiliser made from bird droppings.

☆ WHY DO SOME COUNTRIES HAVE LITTLE FOOD AND OTHERS HAVE PLENTY?

This is also linked with imports and exports. The ability to grow, buy and sell food can mean the difference between having plenty to eat or starving to death. The world's farmers produce enough food to feed the whole planet. But, the food does not get shared out fairly. In the 1980s, the West was producing so much food that it resulted in 'food mountains'. Governments responded by paying farmers not to produce anything the following year.

WHAT PEOPLE EAT MAY DEPEND ON TRADITION AND WHAT IS AVAILABLE	
COUNTRY	**DELICACY**
BOTSWANA	BOILED OR FRIED WORMS
BURMA	GRASSHOPPER KEBABS
MEXICO	ROAST IGUANA
SOUTHERN AUSTRALIA	KANGAROO STEAKS
SIBERIA	REINDEER TONGUE
CHINA	BIRD'S NEST SOUP
ZAIRE	WHITE-NOSED MONKEY STEW
FRANCE	PICKLED SNAILS

☆ WHAT CAN CAUSE FOOD TO BE SCARCE?

1 **CLIMATE** HOT COUNTRIES SUFFER FROM VERY DRY CONDITIONS, CALLED DROUGHTS. LITTLE RAIN FALLS IN THE YEAR, CAUSING CROPS TO FAIL. THIS CAN LEAD TO MASS STARVATION, OR FAMINE.

2 **ECONOMY** IN RUSSIA FOOD IS EXPENSIVE, BECAUSE LITTLE IS PRODUCED THERE, OR IMPORTED AND EXPORTED. CHOICE IS LIMITED AND PEOPLE SPEND HOURS QUEUEING FOR BASICS SUCH AS BREAD, POTATOES AND MILK.

3 **WAR** DURING WORLD WAR II, IT WAS TOO DANGEROUS AND EXPENSIVE TO PRODUCE OR IMPORT MUCH FOOD. PEOPLE WERE GIVEN RATION BOOKS. EACH TOKEN IN THE BOOK COULD BE EXCHANGED FOR FOOD.

4 **LAND** MUCH OF THE LAND IN DEVELOPING COUNTRIES IS OF POOR QUALITY. THE EFFECTS OF CLIMATE AND OVER-FARMING MEAN LAND HAS ALMOST NO NUTRIENTS LEFT. EACH YEAR FEWER CROPS CAN BE GROWN IN THE SOIL.

☆ THE ANSWERS TO THE PROVE IT! ARE: AUSTRALIA: WOOL; INDIA: TEA; JAPAN: ELECTRICAL GOODS.

QUESTION

44 Who rules the world?

No single person or group governs the world. In question 29, we looked at individuals who have power to influence the lives of other people. Groups of people also hold power and often exist to keep the peace between people.

The World

UNITED NATIONS

WHEN FORMED? 1945, AS WORLD WAR II ENDED.

WHY FORMED? TO PROMOTE INTERNATIONAL PEACE AND SECURITY FOR THE COUNTRIES OF THE WORLD AND TO ENCOURAGE COOPERATION BETWEEN THEM.

WHO BELONGS TO THE UN? NEARLY EVERY NATION IN THE WORLD. THERE ARE 159 MEMBER COUNTRIES.

NATO
NORTH ATLANTIC TREATY ORGANISATION

WHEN FORMED? 1949, FOUR YEARS AFTER THE END OF WORLD WAR II.

WHY FORMED? ORIGINALLY TO DEFEND EUROPE AND THE NORTH ATLANTIC AGAINST THE THREAT OF SOVIET AGGRESSION.

WHO BELONGS TO NATO? CANADA, THE USA, AND 13 EUROPEAN COUNTRIES, INCLUDING BELGIUM, DENMARK, PORTUGAL AND THE UNITED KINGDOM.

⬆ United Nations peace-keeping soldiers patrol a market in Sarajevo, Bosnia, in 1993.

EUROPEAN UNION (EU)
THIS USED TO BE CALLED THE EUROPEAN COMMUNITY (EC)

WHEN FORMED? THE EC WAS FORMED IN 1967, WHEN THE EUROPEAN ECONOMIC COMMUNITY (EEC), EUROPEAN ATOMIC ENERGY COMMUNITY (EURATOM) AND THE EUROPEAN COAL AND STEEL COMMUNITY JOINED TOGETHER. THE EC BECAME KNOWN AS THE EU ON 1 NOVEMBER 1993.

WHY FORMED? TO ENCOURAGE COOPERATION BETWEEN MEMBER COUNTRIES AND COMMON AGRICULTURAL AND TRADE POLICIES.

WHO BELONGS TO THE EU? THERE ARE CURRENTLY 15 EUROPEAN MEMBERS. BRITAIN JOINED THE EEC IN 1973.

Individual Countries

Most countries are ruled by large organisations called governments.

☆ THE HISTORY OF GOVERNMENT

PRIMITIVE GROUPS, OR TRIBES, CONSISTED OF SEVERAL FAMILIES AND USUALLY HAD A LEADER. DECISIONS THAT NEEDED TO BE MADE WERE BASED ON CUSTOM AND SUPERSTITION.

BY 3500BC, SOME VILLAGES HAD GROWN INTO SMALL CITIES. GOVERNMENTS WERE CREATED TO PROVIDE SERVICES FOR THE COMMUNITIES. MANY ANCIENT RULERS WERE ALSO RELIGIOUS LEADERS, BUT, THROUGH TIME, EMPERORS, KINGS AND OTHER LEADERS TOOK OVER, CREATING LAWS AND RULES FOR THE PEOPLE.

THE FIRST DEMOCRATIC GOVERNMENT WAS SET UP IN 300BC IN GREECE. MEN COULD VOTE AND PASS LAWS IN THE ASSEMBLY. WOMEN AND SLAVES COULD NOT.

☆ THE BRITISH PARLIAMENT

The British Parliament grew out of a council of noblemen and religious clergy, whose job it was to advise the king. By the late 1700s Parliament had been enlarged to include individuals elected by the people to represent them.

TODAY THE BRITISH GOVERNMENT CONSISTS OF:
● **THE KING OR QUEEN** A ROYAL NON-ELECTED HEAD OF STATE. THEY REPRESENT THE COUNTRY ABROAD, AND HAVE FEW REAL POWERS.
● **THE HOUSE OF COMMONS** 650 POLITICIANS WHO ARE ELECTED BY THE REST OF THE COUNTRY. THE COMMONS DRAWS UP ALL THE LAWS AND REGULATIONS TO GOVERN THE COUNTRY.
● **THE HOUSE OF LORDS** OVER 1,000 NON-ELECTED MEMBERS. THE LORDS HAVE THE POWER TO AMEND ANY LAWS SUGGESTED BY THE COMMONS.
● THE GOVERNMENT IS LED BY AN ELECTED LEADER, CALLED THE **PRIME MINISTER**.
● THE GOVERNMENT MEETS IN THE **HOUSES OF PARLIAMENT**, LONDON. THIS WAS BUILT IN 1834.

☆ THE US CONGRESS

By the end of the 1700s the American Colonies had gained their independence, becoming the United States of America. The US Congress was set up in 1787.

THE US CONGRESS IS MADE UP OF TWO HOUSES:
1 THE UPPER HOUSE (OR **SENATE**). THIS IS MADE UP OF TWO MEMBERS FOR EACH STATE OF AMERICA, ELECTED BY THE PEOPLE. EACH MEMBER IS IN POWER FOR SIX YEARS AND THEN HAS TO BE RE-ELECTED.
2 THE LOWER HOUSE (OR **HOUSE OF REPRESENTATIVES**). THIS IS MADE UP OF 435 MEMBERS, WHO ARE RE-ELECTED EVERY TWO YEARS.
● THE ELECTED HEAD OF THE USA IS CALLED THE **PRESIDENT**.
● THE OFFICIAL RESIDENCE OF THE PRESIDENT IS THE **WHITE HOUSE**, WHICH IS IN WASHINGTON DC. IT WAS BUILT IN 1792-1799.

45 What is democracy?

The word 'democracy' comes from the Greek words 'demos', which means people, and 'kratos', which means rule. So democracy means 'rule by the people'.

IN A DEMOCRATIC SOCIETY...
- EVERY PERSON HAS A SAY IN HOW THEY ARE GOVERNED.
- PEOPLE TAKE PART IN ELECTIONS TO VOTE FOR WHO THEY WOULD LIKE TO REPRESENT THEM IN GOVERNMENT.
- VOTERS HAVE A CHOICE OF SEVERAL POLITICAL PARTIES.

☆ WHO INVENTED DEMOCRACY?

The idea of democracy began in Ancient Greece, where political thinkers believed that people should be ruled by laws that were created by the male citizens.

In the Middle Ages (AD 400s to 1500s) Christianity taught people that every person was equal before God.

In America, the Declaration of Independence, adopted by the Congress in 1776, stressed the importance of the rights of the people of America. In the French Revolution, which began in 1789, great thinkers, such as Voltaire and Rousseau argued for individual rights for all people.

In Russia, in 1917, Soviets were set up. Workers, soldiers and peasants shared control of their country. This experiment in democracy failed because the country was poor and at war, and Stalin's Communist Party dictatorship took over.

After the Industrial Revolution in the 19th century, British people demanded democracy, but it was not until 1918 that all men could take part in voting for a government of their choice. Although Suffragettes actively demonstrated for women's right to vote, they did not win their fight in Britain until 1928.

☆ WHAT IS COMMUNISM AND WHOSE IDEA WAS IT?

IN AN IDEAL COMMUNIST SOCIETY...
- EACH PERSON CONTRIBUTES WHAT THEY CAN ACCORDING TO THEIR ABILITY, AND TAKES FROM SOCIETY ACCORDING TO THEIR NEEDS.
- FARMS, FACTORIES, SCHOOLS AND HOSPITALS ARE OWNED BY THE STATE.
- THERE IS ONLY ONE POLITICAL PARTY – THE COMMUNIST PARTY.

COMMUNISM MEANS 'BELONGING TO ALL'.

IN 1848, KARL MARX AND FRIEDRICH ENGELS WROTE THE COMMUNIST MANIFESTO. IN THE 19TH CENTURY, WORKERS IN EUROPE WERE POORLY TREATED BY THEIR BOSSES. MARX BELIEVED THAT PROPERTY AND WEALTH SHOULD BE SHARED BY THE PEOPLE, AND THAT WORKERS SHOULD NOT BE DOMINATED BY A 'RULING CLASS'. IN THE RUSSIAN REVOLUTION OF 1917, THE BOLSHEVIKS TOOK CONTROL OF RUSSIA, SETTING UP A COMMUNIST GOVERNMENT FOR THE SOVIET UNION. AFTER WORLD WAR II, THE SOVIET ARMIES HELPED TO FREE COUNTRIES, SUCH AS CZECHOSLOVAKIA, EAST GERMANY AND POLAND. HERE THEY SET UP COMMUNIST-CONTROLLED GOVERNMENTS.

➡ BY 1989, MANY COMMUNIST COUNTRIES BEGAN TO FEEL THAT COMMUNISM WAS NOT WORKING. IN POLAND, THE POLITICAL PARTY SOLIDARITY TOOK CONTROL. LECH WALESA IS THE PRESIDENT.

☆ THE WORLD'S LARGEST ELECTION TOOK PLACE IN INDIA IN 1991, WHEN OVER 315 MILLION PEOPLE CAST THEIR VOTES.

46 What is racism?

Racism is a belief that some people are superior to others.

RACISM MAY BE BASED AROUND A NUMBER OF AREAS, FOR EXAMPLE...
- SKIN COLOUR (IN THE SOUTH AFRICAN APARTHEID SYSTEM).
- RELIGION (THE NAZIS' ANTI-SEMITISM, WHICH ENCOURAGED THE MURDER OF JEWISH PEOPLE IN WORLD WAR II).

☆ HAS RACISM ALWAYS EXISTED?

PREJUDICE HAS ALWAYS EXISTED AND THERE ARE MANY EXAMPLES OF RACISM THROUGHOUT HISTORY.
- TRAVELLERS THROUGHOUT HISTORY HAVE BEEN QUICK TO BRAND NATIVE PEOPLE AS 'SAVAGES', MAKING IT EASIER TO CONTROL THEM, AS THEY ARGUED THAT THEY COULD NOT LOOK AFTER THEMSELVES.
- THE SLAVE TRADES IN AFRICA BETWEEN THE 15TH AND 19TH CENTURIES PROMOTED THE IDEA THAT PEOPLE COULD BE OWNED. EUROPEAN TRADERS SHIPPED OVER ABOUT 12 MILLION SLAVES TO WORK ON PLANTATIONS AND MINES IN THE CARIBBEAN AND NORTH AMERICA.

Today different countries have laws making it illegal to treat someone unfairly because of their race, colour or religion. But, racism still exists, because people blame others for taking their land, jobs, homes, food., and their opportunities.

Connect!

HOW CAN WE LEARN MORE ABOUT PEOPLE AND THEIR CULTURES? TURN TO Q47.

QUESTION

47 How can we learn more about each other?

In the past, the only way to learn about people in far-off countries was from the tales of merchants and explorers. These stories were not always true or accurate. Today, things are very different.

☆ WE KNOW MORE ABOUT THE WORLD'S PEOPLE TODAY BECAUSE...

1 We can travel more quickly and more cheaply than ever before.

2 Newspapers, television, radio and films help to increase our knowledge of how we all live.

3 Immigration and emigration spread the ideas of cultures and religions from one country to another.

GROUPS OF PEOPLE JOIN TOGETHER TO CREATE COMMUNITIES, WHICH HAVE THEIR OWN DISTINCT SOCIETIES DEPENDING ON TRADITIONS, CUSTOMS, CIRCUMSTANCES AND ENVIRONMENT.

☆ THERE ARE MANY DIFFERENT WAYS THAT PEOPLE CAN ORGANISE THEMSELVES AS A GROUP OR SOCIETY...

HUNTER-GATHERERS

CASE STUDY
PYGMIES OF CENTRAL AFRICA

Pygmies live in small groups of about 100 people. All their needs are met by the forests they live in. The men hunt for meat, while the women gather nuts, berries and fruit. They live in simple homes made from branches and foliage.

NOMADS

CASE STUDY
BEDOUIN OF ARABIA

The desert is a harsh and barren environment, so the Bedouin live a nomadic existence. This means they are constantly on the move to find new pastures and watering holes. Their tents are easily taken down and carried on camel-back to the next site.

FARMERS

CASE STUDY
RICE-GROWERS OF CHINA

China's high rainfall and fertile soil make it ideal for growing rice. People tend to settle in one place and work in the fields. The farmers have a strong sense of belonging because the location of the rice fields always remains fixed.

CITY DWELLERS

CASE STUDY
NEW YORKERS

Most people who earn a living work for part of the week and relax during the rest. Although many people like to spend money on their home, cars and leisure activities, a city is made up of people with different opinions, ideas and desires.

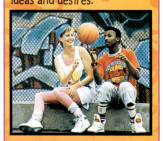

☆ AROUND 80% OF THE WORLD'S POPULATION ARE FARMERS AND 20% LIVE IN TOWNS. 0.5% ARE NOMADS OR HUNTER-GATHERERS.

QUESTION 48

How do nations communicate with each other?

Communication technology is advancing all the time. We can now contact someone halfway round the globe in an instant.

EXAMINE THIS HISTORY OF COMMUNICATION...

1837 = FIRST BRITISH ELECTRIC TELEGRAPH.
1866 = TELEGRAPH TRANSMITS MESSAGES FROM BRITAIN TO AMERICA.
1876 = ALEXANDER BELL INVENTS THE TELEPHONE.
1895 = GUGLIELMO MARCONI TRANSMITS RADIO SIGNALS OVER A MILE.
1901 = MARCONI SENDS RADIO SIGNALS ACROSS THE ATLANTIC.
1926 = SCOTSMAN JOHN LOGIE BAIRD INVENTS THE TELEVISION.
1928 = FIRST TRANSATLANTIC TELEPHONE.
1962 = COMMUNICATIONS SATELLITE IN SPACE BEAMS TV AND RADIO SIGNALS ALL OVER THE WORLD.
1970 = FIBRE OPTICS TRANSMIT TELEPHONE MESSAGES ACROSS THE GLOBE IN MERE SECONDS.

QUESTION 49

Are there any people on Earth who are unaware of the rest of civilisation?

Probably not, although some remote mountain regions and denser parts of the rainforests remain unexplored.

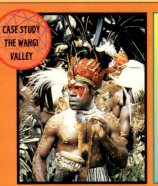

CASE STUDY THE WAHGI VALLEY

THE WAHGI VALLEY IS IN THE MOUNTAINS OF PAPUA NEW GUINEA. NO-ONE KNEW THERE WAS ANYONE LIVING THERE UNTIL 1933, WHEN A GROUP OF AUSTRALIAN EXPLORERS STUMBLED ACROSS THE AREA. WHEN THE WAHGI FIRST SAW THESE EXPLORERS SOME OF THEM THOUGHT THEY WERE THEIR OWN RELATIVES RETURNED FROM THE DEAD. THE WAHGI WERE LIVING A SIMPLE LIFE, FARMING FOR FOOD, MAKING TOOLS FROM STONE AND CLOTHES FROM PLANT FIBRES. THEY TRADED BY BARTERING WITH AXES, SHELL ORNAMENTS AND PIGS. TODAY, ALTHOUGH THEY HAVE NOT ABANDONED ALL THEIR TRADITIONS, THEIR COFFEE BEAN FARMING HAS BECOME PART OF THE INTERNATIONAL ECONOMY.

QUESTION 50

And how do we deal with death?

Different cultures treat death in very different ways.

☆ **IS DEATH ALWAYS A SAD TIME?**

NO. IN MEXICO, THEY HAVE A SPECIAL 'DAY OF THE DEAD' FESTIVAL ON THE FIRST DAY OF NOVEMBER. INSTEAD OF MOURNING THE DEAD, PEOPLE CELEBRATE THEM. THEY MAKE GIFTS OF SWEETS, FRUITS AND FLOWERS TO WELCOME THE SOULS OF THE DEAD BACK TO THEIR FAMILIES.

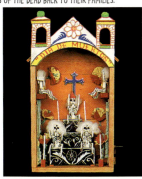

● **BURIAL** JEWS, MUSLIMS AND MANY CHRISTIANS BURY THEIR DEAD. JEWS ARE BURIED WITH THEIR HEADS FACING JERUSALEM. MUSLIMS ALSO FACE THEIR HOLY CITY, WHICH IS MECCA, IN SAUDI ARABIA.

● **CREMATION** SIKHS, HINDUS AND BUDDHISTS BURN THE BODIES OF THE DEAD. THIS IS CALLED CREMATION. HINDUS IN INDIA SCATTER THE ASHES OVER THE RIVER GANGES, WHOSE WATERS ARE BELIEVED TO BE SACRED.

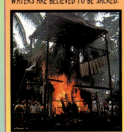

● SOME PEOPLE HAVE THEIR BODIES FROZEN AFTER THEY DIE. THE BODIES ARE STORED IN SPECIAL FREEZERS. THEIR HOPE IS THAT MEDICAL ADVANCES IN THE FUTURE WILL BE ABLE TO BRING THEM BACK TO LIFE.

Connections!

People all over the globe have different needs, beliefs and ways of living. It is up to each individual to be aware of how their actions affect the people around them and the world as a whole. 🟠

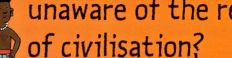

Connections!
PEOPLE
Index